T0162356

NEAR
SOLSTICE

ALSO BY MADELON SPRENGNETHER:

POETRY

The Angel of Duluth (2006)

The Normal Heart (1981)

MEMOIR

Great River Road: Memoir and Memory (2015)

Crying at the Movies (2002)

Rivers, Stories, Houses, Dreams (1983)

WOMEN'S TRAVEL WRITINGS (CO-EDITOR)

The House on Via Gombito (1991, 1997)

NEAR SOLSTICE

Prose Poems by
Madelon
Sprengnether

HOLY COW! PRESS
DULUTH, MINNESOTA
2015

Copyright © 2015 by Madelon Sprengnether.
Author photograph by Michael Young.

All rights reserved. No part of this book may be used
or reproduced in any manner whatsoever without
written permission except in the case of brief quotations
embodied in critical articles and reviews. Printed
and bound in the United States of America.

Book design by Anton Khodakovsky.

First printing, 2015

ISBN 978-0-9859818-9-1

10 9 8 7 6 5 4 3 2 1

This project is supported in part by grant awards from
the Ben and Jeanne Overman Charitable Trust, the
Elmer L. and Eleanor J. Andersen Foundation, the
Cy and Paula DeCosse Fund of The Minneapolis
Foundation, and by gifts from individual donors.

Holy Cow! Press books are distributed to the trade by
Consortium Book Sales & Distribution, c/o Perseus
Distribution, 210 American Drive, Jackson, TN 38301.

For inquiries, please write to: Holy Cow!
Press, Post Office Box 3170, Mount Royal
Station, Duluth, MN 55803.

Visit www.holycowpress.org

Acknowledgements

"Hands," "Skin," and "Drowning in air" appeared in *Women's Studies*, vol. 31, no. 4 (July-August, 2002), 523-24.

"August," "Leda at the lake," "Like a painting by Edward Hopper" and "Green" appeared in *The North Stone Review*, no.14, 273-76.

"Sauna" was published on March 20, 2008 on the website FLURRY, www.toddbosspoet.com/Flurry/Flurry.html.

The following poems appeared in *Near Solstice, Mourning,* a chapbook published by West Town Press, 2009: "Near solstice," "Landscape," "Ash Wednesday," "Hospital," "Sauna," "Heat," "Skin," "Fluids," "Hands," "Sinews," "Heart," "Sarasota," "Surf," "Half Moon Bay," "Jungle Gardens," "Spanish Point," "Drowning in Air," "In May," "Like a painting by Edward Hopper" and "Green."

Table of Contents

For Roberta Lucas Sprengnether
(1916–1998)

NEAR SOLSTICE

Near solstice

But not quite. Toward sunset it's pale, peachy, more a
glow than a color. How everything shines. As if we were
nearing the end of days, scuffing through leaves so dry
they ought not to look like something about to rise.
Thinking about my mother's grave, the earth roughed
up around a hole in the ground. It was raining when we
left, though gingko leaves stuck to our shoes, like fans
of beaten gold. My brother won't blame the river for
taking our father's life. Nor me—gazing at the branches
of trees dancing in water. But I'd go back. To push the
damp earth away with my hands. Wanting more. Light.

Landscape

There's a lavender light, on an overcast day just after dawn, in January. Something like fog, shrouding everything familiar. Trees line the street, dressed in black, like an act of contrition. You don't live here. Not in this haze of dirty snow, beautiful only in its air of reproach. Like a lover who turns and walks away in one of those grainy, East European movies. It is too quiet—when what you want is a wail, thin and ecstatic. Like a psalmist's note.

Ash Wednesday

A phone call wakes me. I don't recognize his voice. Right
away, I apologize. "I have bad news," he says. Cutting
right in. The first thing I know this morning is that my
brother has cancer. There must be another way to say
this. How suddenly a mid-February day seems gray and
cindery. How even the lightly falling snow looks like
someone's bones fired to ash. How I hesitate to walk
in it. How I heard once that Diego Rivera ingested the
remains of Frieda Kahlo, his wife. Her dust. His dust.

Hospital

You might be your mother. Walking the linoleum-tiled corridors of this hospital, following the yellow arrows to your routine test. Comparing your condition to everyone you pass—in wheelchairs, with oxygen masks, in blue cotton gowns, on gurneys with IVs attached. How she hated this, recoiling from the less fortunate. Those who couldn't or wouldn't be going home. Safe in your daughterhood, you identified with those who escape. Your mother dead, you inhale the breathy odor of her fear. Like tongues of ravening dogs at your feet.

Sauna

Lying on the upper shelf, I stare at the walls and ceiling.
Gray tile slanting one way, white tile the other. A smudgy
line of caulk—like a finger pressed along a seam—which
is not smooth, but nubbly. As if it, too, were sweating.
Another skin raised and pulsing with the heat. One
sits, one reclines, one hunches over herself. Women
like odalisques. Slight crackling of coals, hiss of steam
rising. Here, now. What you feel. Heat. Gray wall, white
wall, glaze of pale flesh. Wintry wash of indoor light.

Heat

Is heat a form of love? How it clings to you, touching you all over, not disdaining your most intimate, even smelly places. Your mouth, stale from too many cups of coffee, your underarms sweaty from the stress-a-climber and the rowing machine, your ass and your cunt—well because you haven't showered since morning, and it's your ass and your cunt. Heat slimes against your skin, mingling with your own juices. Like the way you get wet before sex. How you can't keep to yourself. Helpless and spilling—better than any human covenant—is this the way God speaks to us?

Skin

What are you but layers of cells—in an unstable order? Easily bruised, chafed, abraded, reddened, inflamed, burned. Spotty, freckled, mole-ridden, hairy. Flinching at the least sign of exposure. Yet you make your own envelope, sleek and silky, by liquefying. When my body weeps or perspires, I feel cared for. What is the source of your bodywaters? Is there a ground table of sweat and tears, some headstream from which all tributaries flow? Skin you are much too unsolid. What do you know how to do but let the outside in, the inside out?

Fluids

Sweat prickles up the back of my neck, pooling in the
shadowy crevices of my body. Blood leaks and clots. Tears
seep from the corners of my eyes, calcifying on my cheeks.
Everything I try to hold inside. All that the mouth receives,
contains or swallows. What the stomach churns, what the
short intestine siphons and refines. Mucus, signifying the
warm dampness necessary to life. Tasting of yeast, iron
and salt, the slippery parts of me tell my body's story. They
speak of drought or plenty. They say how wet or dry I am.

Hands

What have I ever liked about them? My fingers long-boned and twiggy, encased in gristle. Thin, yellow ridges below my digits, attesting to the strength of my grip. Veins protruding like something obscene, mapping the susurrus of my blood. Skin so fine-lined from folding and creasing (like a letter from loving or obsessive reading) that it will never be smoothed flat. Cuticles ragged and sometimes bleeding, nails rippled like a beast with a horn—at least I don't chew them. Hands, how exposed you are. How public.

Sinews

I am in love with the elastic tissue of my body, with its supple, fibrous pulse. These are tendons, long, nerve-like, and well, sinewy. She has nerve, we say, or she is nervy, or she is on the verge of a nervous breakdown. When I cut a piece of raw chicken I can see them—thin and white, impossible to sever with a single stroke of the knife. Am I, too, like this? Something like bamboo roots, tough and stringy—the kind of twisted rope an Atropos might weave. Today, I am feeling my joints and sinews, how smoothly they articulate. How jumbled my chalky bones without their sweet caress. How lonely. Inert.

Heart

Sometimes on the rowing machine, I close my eyes,
feeling my body elongate and scrunch. First hard pull,
then swoosh—like a single muscle. This is your work,
as obvious as weight, pressure or sweat. I saw it once, on
the ultrasound screen, how smoothly you perform your
slippery isotonics. And fell in love with your long-distance
running. How you trip in place to your own rap beat.
First contraction, then rhythm, visceral and urgent—like
eating or sex. As stark as an infant's first slap of oxygen.
As grave as an amphibious creature's first breath.

SARASOTA

Sarasota

The air here is salty and wet—as close to my skin as hand in glove, flesh against flesh. I expand to fill this space. Even my hair flares up—alive and snaky. In the water, I float, my whole, long body buoyant and bobbing. When I open my eyes, everything is blue-green and shimmery. I must have known this once—how to rock and sway in warm, amniotic currents. Some species can do this. They dive and rise, expelling air in a spume of light. The simplest things speak to us. The surf a persistent, messy kind of love. My own pale torso and limbs fluid all of a sudden. Fishlike.

Surf

Immersed. A thick, tart taste in my mouth. No horizon, only a haze of turquoise, fading into blue. Maybe a change of texture. Like taffeta—stiff, a little ruffled—against smooth, unblemished silk. Whole families float off-shore, children clinging to their parents' shoulders. Farther out, a speedboat whomps by, churning up froth. The surf, that anonymous heavy-breather, thrashes against my ears at night. Is this what I will remember? Or the evening I sat on the beach, watching a man flash a light for his son through the warm-tongued waves at the shore. A neon, moon-shape of tears.

Half Moon Bay

A little beach, horseshoe shaped, flanked by bigger, more
serious hotels. The Adirondack chairs, at night, look
whitish, skeletal. Piers jut forward in the shape of prows,
with round lollipop lights on sticks. Pulses of lightning
flash through the sky—the throb of a distant migraine. Is
this a painting by Dali or De Chirico? By day, the water
is lime-green, lit by the ground-up glitter of shell below.
It rains, sometimes, with monsoon force. Proving that
everything, solid or liquid, is bound to transubstantiate?
Like steam rising from hot asphalt. Or the tears I can't hold
back that slime and sting. As luminous as snail tracks.

Jungle Gardens

I learn that snakes can't see too well, can't hear at all. They
go by heat and motion, flashing their forked tongues at us.
A trainer, who carries a black snake coiled around his arm,
warns about the beautiful, venomous coral—as likely as
not to appear in your back yard. It's tricky to know what's
what when an alligator, used to a diet of marshmallows, will
snap up a three-year-old so fast no one notices. Slithering
into the bulrushes. The same that Miriam wove into a cradle
for her brother. The same the Egyptians beat into another
purpose—pounding its pith to a fine, linen-like surface. So
they could tell us what they had? Or what they had lost.

Spanish Point

"Midden," the archeologist's term for trash heap or garbage
dump. Here at Spanish Point, the place where prehistoric
Indians left the stuff they couldn't use or didn't want.
Shell, flint, and broken ceramic. Layers of grit and mud.
Century after century, in the same spot. We pick it apart—
to know what they wore, what they ate, what they needed,
what they tossed. It looks the same as earth from above.
Underneath, decades of debris, secretive and dense. Like
the surprise I found in my basement when I removed
an old, musty carpet. A ring of stone at the center. Like
a well, a cesspool, some kind of hearth, or burial pit.

Drowning in air

This is called "sugar sand." A fine, powdery substance that clings to wet skin, like bone meal, or ash. Little, minnowy fish near the shore. Sting rays, too, seeking shallow water to mate. Toward the end, my mother's lungs kept filling with fluid, like water-logged cork. While the oxygen concentrator bubbled and droned, she swam through seaweed, struggling for breath. When her toes began to blister and ooze, her caregiver said she'd seen this before—it was "all that liquid trying to come out." I am heading straight into the Gulf, opening my eyes underwater, aiming for something other than sky. My mother was drowning in air.

In May

Something is wrong with this landscape. Everything's too
green. After winter's strict discipline—all the colors it gave
up—I can't help but disbelieve. Like baby's flesh, such
newness is painful to contemplate. Doesn't anything exposed
like that hurt? The dirty snow got so hard by the end—like
styrofoam painted with concrete. Winter's pitted pores and
blackhead-spotted skin. I'd scuff my boots against the ice,
pull my coat tighter against the wind. In late spring I forget
everything I know about trees. Their heedless punctual life.

Like a painting by Edward Hopper

All day you feel uneasy, blessed. You feel clouds passing, their speed, their density. Like a painting by Edward Hopper, sinister and seductive. Or some cryptic accord between moon and sun. Who is observing you? Is it your time yet? Later, you count the seconds between lightning and thunder. You know how quickly—like kerosene soaked rags or tinder—*you* would ignite. How the wand of the maple tree in your yard, shaking to its roots, loves this. How green goes all dark and shadowy sometimes. How it rains then in swift Samurai sheets.

Green

Is it fat? Is it juicy? Is it lush? Is it humid, like the wetness
that exudes from warm skin? Like a body overflowing
its boundaries and pressing against your very flesh? Is it
soft like a billowy parachute, so you want to fall into it, a
skydiver plummeting? At night is it wavy and breathy and
dark, an ambiguous lover? Will you murmur your sorrows,
your lips wet with kisses? Will you sing to it, calling and
calling? Will you drench yourself in its shimmery odor, like
a summer downpour? Will you confess all your faults? Can
you believe in something as greedy and repetitive as green?

LEDA AT THE LAKE

Serving

My mother would sit in her wheelchair by the breakfast
table, while my brother bent over her feet. Unwinding the
bandages from her blistered and infected toes. Her skin was
mottled and taut—her feet so stiff she could barely stand.
Moving from bed to chair and back again. My brother applied
antiseptic ointment to her open sores—wrapping them in
gauze before leaving for work. "I was in a hurry," he said,
"and afraid I'd be late." I think of him now. On his knees, his
glasses slipping forward, his tie dipping into the basin, as he
lifts first one foot, then the other. Breathing a little hard.

Attending
(for my former mother-in-law)

I'm the attendant, the one who stands like a sentinel, ready to help. Who gives directions like "I think you're supposed to take your sleeping pill while you're sitting up." Who tries to disengage your stiff, bent arm before lifting the dress over your head. Who holds the drain for the catheter bag. Who measures your urine before pouring it into the toilet. I'm not the one who kneels on the floor to remove your shoes or your molded leg brace. Who turns and eases your body onto the mattress. I don't look at your breasts with their surprising pink tips. It's my grown-up daughter who does this.

Lola

You're awake. Your hair swept thinly away from your face—
your skin pale and crinkled, like nubby silk. No lipstick,
no rouge. I kiss your cheek, pick up your hand, rubbing it
with two fingers. Of course you know me, you shout—at
the nurse who hovers on the blurry edge of your vision. I
find water for the flowers I brought, unwrap my present, a
4x6 photo of three. You, me and my mother. You ask me to
search for the book you lost—with all the names you want to
recall—somewhere in the jumble of cards and faded blooms.
There, on that table! A place infinitely far across the room.

2

I'm here with good intentions. You'll get better, return to your apartment, outwit your illness—at least for another year. Not like my mother, gasping, speechless. But today, your mouth is slack, your words slurred. Your dinner sliding down your chin, puddling in the creases of your gown. Mush. I scurry into the bathroom, holding my long-fingered hands under the tap to take the chill off. Then wipe your face and neck with a soft washcloth. "There," I say, "would you like some dessert now?" Pushing the Jello closer to the front of the tray. So I can scrutinize each bite. As you lift one shivery spoonful after another to your mouth.

Lago Mar

Lake/sea. Causeway and river between. Refuge from early
northern/Midwestern winter—twenty degrees colder this
year. Two pools, blue-green and sinuous, tennis courts, volley
ball, boats for hire, exotic finger-foods, and pink or lime-
colored drinks. Saturated salt-sea air. A small infection on
your thumb that swells and stings. Don't bacteria thrive here
also? Pulsating rhythm that interrupts sleep—like a digital
alarm. A trick of consciousness/deep-sea fish flying out of
the oily Atlantic. Everyone you've ever loved/sidling up to
you in the dark/laying their dying wishes on the shore.

2

Here in the palm tree shadows and the dark, sipping a
Manhattan, as two women swim in the warm, illuminated
pool. One does a breast-stroke, while the other walks
the bottom, lifting and dipping her arms in a simple,
freestyle motion. Toward me and away and back again—
not watching me watching them—in such earnest
conversation. Not knowing that someone I care for
has died. News splashed, like fresh blood, over the TV
screen in my room. Lying here, obscured from view,
like an off-cast member of a movie-scene. Observing
two women in the privacy and luxury of their swim.

Racoon

It died at the foot of my steps. As if it had trudged up the
steamy asphalt hill to pause at the stone slab, resting its belly
against the cool, dark slate. How to dispose of it? Lift it by the
tail, carry it to the garbage bin? What if it's diseased? Rabid.
Yet it looks innocuous, lying peacefully on its side. Perhaps
if I go away for a while, it will get up and saunter off. Later in
the day, it's still there—only altered. In the bearing-down sun,
it has rolled onto its back. Like a bad taxidermy job. Showing
its snarl of perfect teeth. Its stiff sex, its puffed-out ass.

2

How can I sleep? I double-lock the door and clamp the windows shut. But his summer-sick smell penetrates wood and glass. Flesh swelling, fluids leaking into the gutter. A ripened, hairy obscenity. Who is responsible? The moon, big, round and impassive, won't help. Reeking and unattended, his body drives me to act. My tools crude, sharp and improvised at this hour—my aim no higher than any woman's. To cover him. His glazed astonishment. With anything I can find. A garden shovel. A dark sack.

Leda at the lake

Nothing fancy about this lake. Mid-town, a few trees, the
ground weedy and hard, littered with dog turds. Here
I am, a middle-aged woman, slathered in Coppertone,
lying on a striped beach towel. Propped on one elbow,
trying to read, or at least get a tan. It's no use. I'm too hot.
I go for a swim, wading in, splashing water against my
arms, launching myself breast first, pushing the wetness
away with my hands. I fear the water the way I fear God.
All around you and so ambiguous. I lumber out onto
the sand, my nipples showing against my tank suit, my
thighs looking bigger than I remember. Tonight, I'll sleep
heavily in my warm skin. Next to an open window.

Golden door

"We'll meet," my friend assured her mother "behind the golden door." Here's one—in a sculpture garden—made of wood wrapped with mylar. Like something you could actually walk through. But it's smooth and hard to the touch, forcing you back onto the path. You almost admire the way it resists, how all it reveals is yourself—incoherent. The golden floor is slick also, a gleaming boardwalk under a hedge too low for entry. There's only one place you can stand. Under the pine tree with strips of gold tied to its boughs. Like salamanders' tails—whipping in the fiery afternoon sun.

August

This dusk is blue-bottle green. Water pattering over the garden in soft sibilances, like the voices of mother and father sifting under the bedroom door, or light from a distant room in the deep, late hours of childish terror. How many drift-down layers to this day. Waking through mists of dreams, like veils of fog wrapping my face, dispersing later at the insistence of sun. Sinking again, midday, into sleep-soaked euphoria, in which I bear my burdens (like bleached and fallen trees) as lightly as tinder. Waking again to a landscape of change. To green growing darker, a sound like bullets of acorns falling—chirr of crickets, first startlings of rain.

ST. FRANCIS

St. Francis

Dying, he knew what to do. Calling his brothers to him,
stretching his arms in helpless abandon. He wasn't afraid
of suffering, having prayed for and gotten the stigmata.
Abscessed wounds that refused to heal. Like cancer.
Death, he believed, held no surprises, being a state of no
separation. What he didn't bargain for was us. The dumb
spectators. What if we look away or fall asleep? Worse,
suppose we do something that hastens the end? How can
we bear the change in us? Our hearts—those long-distance
sinners—pumping blood into all our healthy limbs?

Pentecost

It was like this: a private room. Locked. Huddled together, in fear of everything. Quick, warm presence. Rhythm of breathing. Or it could have been: a violent wind. Light flashed into the brainpan. Sounds no one could comprehend. Cacophony. We saw things. A dead man with bleeding hands, the sun gone black, the moon a fiery red. For some, this meant we had to part. For others, we had to be together. Like hearing such a pure and high-pitched note we hated our own voices. Yet each of us began. Annihilating song—our throats scored open.

Reliquary

How physical this story. Born—in the ordinary way—
through sundering flesh. Fed—in the ordinary way—
at a woman's big, brown, upstanding nipples. Yet how
can we be sure? What if it's all made up? We want the
facts ma'am, so here's evidence. Chips of bone in a tiny
glass pane, in a highly wrought piece of silver and gold.
But which ones? A finger knuckle, toe joint, fragment
of slipped disk? And what about that image of his face?
Too small to belong to anyone—even a man of his
time. So tell me. What on earth God wants from us?

God considers his sons Qusay and Uday

I don't recognize you. Pudgy, hairy, bloody and naked. As
boys, you were quick-limbed and such a handful. Running
this way and that and into everything. How long since
we've been in touch? With so many to look after, I confess
I lose track. The sight of you now shocks me. How to
explain that I loved you from the moment you quickened.
As I love everything that generates. Lilies that fester, along
with the weeds. But once you're started, I have to look
elsewhere. Surely, you understand. Yet seeing you now I
feel unaccountably sad. Remembering also my son Che.

God considers the resurrection according to Stanley Spencer

You had partly the right idea—how everything comes back,
no matter how lost, trivial or disgusting. Flies and food
scraps included. And the way you imagine women fondled
by sunflowers—or men tonguing dogs. What a chuckle!
It made perfect sense to plop you down in Cookham—
on the sweet-running Thames. But who since Blake or
John Donne has had such crazy ideas? A regatta where
Jesus preaches to revelers? Well, I'm flattered and choose
to indulge you. So many think me a snob, whereas *you*—
deliver everyone and everything back into my hands.

Stanley Spencer talks back

It was never a sacrilege to paint you. I saw you everywhere—
in tradesmen and butchers—on the streets of Cookham.
Even rising from the local churchyard, pushing the
gravestone away with your hands. You were there also in the
hospital for the insane, when the freshly wounded arrived
from France. You made their beds, emptied their slops, cut
away gangrene. In Macedonia—where soldiers filled water
bottles, cleaned their gear, then lay sleeping on the hillside—
you slept with them. When they dreamed of women,
large-limbed and capacious, making love to anything,
you entered this heaven. You dreamed the same dream.

BODYWORLDS

Bodyworlds

Muscle and ligament—this flesh is dead. Lifted, filleted, separated from bone. Nerves spread. Veins, arteries and capillaries exposed. Clouds of these, tender and red as a radish. A man holds his wife's hand—blood froth of rose. My love is like? What I'd feared. Yet relaxing my hip against yours, my hand sliding down your back, the smooth contour of your buttocks, I'm amazed. Their lives. Ours.

2

So many of these bodies are male. *Plastinated* is the word—
how they are preserved. By consent. No grave robbing here.
But did they know? How I would stare and stare. At the thin
strands of their gonads. A throbbing voyeur. How tender
those threads. How slim and fine their designs on the future.
I didn't know. Had never known. How could I know?

3

The pregnant woman—like an Etruscan funerary statue—
reclines. But sliced apart. Her womb halved like a peach. This
is the exhibit of the unborn. How I remember the swimming
view of my first grandchild—two fists raised on either side of
her skull. These died—every fetus in this room. Who could
have guessed how serene they'd look? As we, the unbeautiful,
file silently past. Pressing our faces closer to the glass.

4

Take hold of me. *Mouth, throat, heart.* Like those who give themselves up to science. *Lungs, stomach, pancreas.* Their bodies no longer individual. I remember how it was once, each organ guarding its secret. *Liver, kidneys, intestines.* Small matters of possession. But you, you pry into me. *Vulva, anus, vagina.* Tight as an oyster.

5

Where is shame? Is there anything left to withhold? My
history as friable as flesh—most quiet of thoughts revealed.
If God were like this, I might love him. But it's you and me.
Gazing at those who've gone before. Later, you put your
hands in my hair as I caress you, loving with my tongue.
Then, grasping my hands in yours—as you come. Hard.

Massage

My hands know you. The rise of your shoulders, the muscles of your arms, the mounds and concavities of your palms, and each long digit. They know the bony protrusions of your vertebrae and the curve of your tailbone. They know the flesh of your cheeks. Your inner thighs, your calves and narrow feet. How you've balanced and stood on each solid heel. How it feels to hold them.

2

My tongue knows you. The rim of your lips and inside
of your mouth—the hard and soft places within. The
twin knots of your nipples, sharp incline of your rib cage,
and swirl of hair below. It knows your size and shape,
how you fit the dimensions of my mouth. The tender
place beneath your balls. The hot dark of your anus.

3

My cunt knows you. How it speaks another language,
babbling against your fingers and tongue. How you enter.
Sudden. Different. Like nothing I know. How everything
is talking—from my secret interior—in syllables
nonsensical. Sweet. Sweeter. Sweetest. Cacophony.

EURYDICE

How amazed

How amazed—at the teeming life around me—I was
when my mother died. Everyone, everywhere was so
alive. Ruddy and confident. On the street, in cars, in the
supermarket, in doctors' waiting rooms, at airports, even
in lines at the post office. No one but me showed surprise.
At this smelly, tangled, fleshy mass. I, instead, considered
the dead. Their gray-white bones. Gravelly ash. How
many—by death—undone. Irresistible their number.

Near death

Near death, do we feel life more acutely? In proximity,
I mean. Near news of my brother slouched at the
breakfast room table in our old house—sliming and
decomposing—I felt at first a pull toward him. Toward
loss of breath. Like a shadow flown to a corner of the
room. My own flesh slack and wrinkled—like a crumpled
party balloon. Later it made me lusty. As if I could push
all my oxygen through his limbs. As if the blood rushing
to my head might also (somehow)? Animate him.

After

Early summer late in the day, sky portending another storm.
My friend from out of town has mowed my grass, taken a
shower, and is sleeping now in the living room. Sitting on
the front porch, paging through a magazine, I look up at
the broad green leaves of the oak in my yard, listen to the
birds they conceal, watch girls across the street take turns
in their jumping rope games. My friend wakes, comes to
the screen door, says it's time to go. A small wind unsettles
the leaves, scatters the girls, makes urgent the birds' song.

2

Death is real. What more can I say? Becoming ever more itself over time. As I age, as my hair thins, my skin pouches and crinkles, death is impervious. Death doesn't care. Only death does not change. And—listen to me—no matter what you've heard, death *is* proud. Trumpeting itself. See, I'm still here! Being dead is no game. Like hide and seek, when all at last are discovered. No matter how dark the summer night, no matter how sinister the trees' swaying leaves. No one is lost. All then—I tell you—all will be found.

Blue–violet light

Blue-violet light at dusk, nearly electric against the snow.
How we need it—even those small, colored bulbs winking
along roof lines or framing dark doorways. Today, I heard
an expert explain how pandemic flu will come. Like 1918.
Birds get it, then we do, passing it from hand to hand. As
fast as light racing around the globe. At yoga tonight, I hold
my arms outstretched, chanting "Ma, ma," focusing on the
closed eye in the middle of my forehead. I fall into Christmas
at age 6, 7, or 8. Before I knew anyone would die. Father,
mother, brother. I imagine them now, reaching toward
me. With their flume-like fingers, their weightless arms.

October fire

Driving along the tree-lined street, littering with leaves.
No words. Though color. Sliding past on either side.
Should notice. Try to. Can't. But yellow. Yellower?
Yellowest? Maybe even—orange, persimmon, tangerine.
October on a spree. Going for broke. A luxury—like
the sun—too dazzling to contemplate. Like a pyre? Or
maybe—Danae. Spreading her thighs. Profligate.

Early December

Early December. Light sliding from the sky and pooling on
the horizon. Too silvery smooth to hold the sun's buttery
wafer. The river below a dull, leaden mirror. Small dark figures
hunched along the walk. Like hunters—or skaters—in a
painting by Breugel. Even you, in your warm car, are barely
discernible. Unlike the sharp stems sticking up from the
snow, the oak trees' tarnished leaves. Persistent hanging gold.

This soft fate

Snow today. First of season. In pale drifts, hushing everything. White, it says, I am white. Unfathomable. You can resist—fingers clenched, capillaries shocked, pushing blood back to your knuckles—as you scrape the ice from your windshield. Sweeping mounds of crystal from the hood of your car. Turning the heat up on high. Or you can give in. Feeling the wheels now slip and swerve. This soft fate. Watching it come down.

Birds

Birds are the background. Alighting on a vine in my
yard, so small I can hardly see them. Gnarls in the wood.
Tiny fists of darkness against the snow. But one twitches
a beak, one settles a wing. Against this brilliance, they
are sentient. Light is a laser, obliterating. Let me live in
umbra instead. Like the moon—pulsing and red—in the
earth's big shadow. Tonight, I will think of you—dots of
resistance. Your hearts, stringy tangle. Beating fast and hot.

Eurydice

I don't know how I fell behind. We were walking side by side. The fields straw-colored at first, then tawny, then raw, golden yellow. I would slow for the gullies, full of waving grasses reaching to my crotch, my waist. Was I foolish? To keep my eyes lowered, gazing only on what lay under foot. Rocks, like ghostly step-stones, across the dry creek. Mud oozing up between. The chirr and rustle as I moved. The light coming down, the light coming up. Everything illumined.

2

What I remember. How you whispered, holding my head, caressing my hair, moving your hands over my shoulders, breasts, rib cage and abdomen. How you moved my legs apart, touching me just there. How you sat up and leaned down—to look, probe, taste. How I moved my hands over your back, making small animal sounds. How you reached back to pull on my nipple. And how you turned, placing both hands on my breasts, pushing into my vulva. Up to the first muscle. Then how I gave way. Again, again, and again.

EL DORADO

El Dorado

November sky—rain-gray clouds with an underwash
of blue. Ghostly trees on the horizon, their twisted,
snaky arms like a fairy tale briar. Or thicket of pubic hair.
Illumination pale and low, close to the ground. Where
color rises up. In fields of uncut grass. Tasselating. Red,
rust, ochre, brown, maroon. There's gold, too, flashed
through. In the car, driving home, I lay my hand on your
thigh, the smooth long muscle that leads to your groin.

2

What is it to dream of gold? Not as a young man—or woman—seeking. Go somewhere. Have something. That we can't anyway hold. West as good as east in the end, and don't they converge? Columbus, Coronado, De Soto. Where you land, does it matter? Here, in the middle of Kansas— like Dorothy bewildered of her home—or elsewhere? What if love really is the answer—like an Oprah Winfrey testimonial or one of those tacky sin and redemption stories?

3

I can't stop seeing. Like some nutty, fucked-up kind of artist.
Say Vincent van Gogh. Or Georgia O'Keeffe. Obsessed
with how things look. How beautiful. Is everydayness.
These trees. This field. The burnished light over naked
ground. Like the etymology of a single word. Its grip,
shift and slur. But when it comes to saying how my body
lies down, I'm speechless. Or trite. Saying oh, oh, oh.
Or yes, yes, yes. Wheels within wheels. Burning.

4

You tell me—in the midst of a massage—how your
father, then your mother, died. Both, long-term smokers.
Your father, you say, lost his mind. Misshapen cells
sifting through his brain. Your mother's death was
more gradual. Rational. And you cared for her. As
she, once, had cared for you. Doing things you had
never thought possible. Between mother and son.

5

If I only knew where we were going. I'd know how to
end. How we each found what we dreamed. In that place
where we lost our way—straying into the many-branched
wood. Where even trees insist on their unwished-for
stories. Instead, all I can say, driving away from El Dorado,
is how quiet, how grateful I am. For light breaking—just
now—through that dense bank of clouds. See there?
White gold. Luminescence. Do you see? Just driving.

Light uprises

Dun-colored trees. Grass cut close, like a marine haircut. Branching low to the ground in star-like clusters that make crunching sounds underfoot. Walking as if on a field of locusts. In the gullies, where secret water flows, bushy things stand up, pricking my face and hands as I part their waving strands. A wind passes over the pond, rippling its skin, like a piece of newly crinkled foil. At the smooth horizon, the sky is nearly indigo. From the broad, tawny-colored field, a light uprises. Shines.

Good Friday, Driving Eastward (after John Donne)

Toward the sun? Or away. In El Dorado that afternoon,
I stood watching it melt down. Or was it us riding the
earth's big shoulders, turning our backs on all that gold?
West our loss, east our destination. The moon, irresistibly
silver, as round as a shiny new coin. Even still, in motion.
Turn slowly now and face the magnificent pyre. Flame
of grass, smudgy tree line, darkness coming. Simplest
of stories. Falling and rising. Away and toward.

About the Author

Madelon Sprengnether is Regents Professor of English at the University of Minnesota, where she teaches in the MFA Program. She is the author of two memoirs, *Rivers, Stories, Houses, Dreams,* and *Crying at the Movies;* two collections of poetry, *The Normal Heart,* and *The Angel of Duluth;* a co-edited collection of women's travel writing, *The House on Via Gombito;* and numerous other works of feminist literary and psychoanalytic scholarship. *The Normal Heart* was a Minnesota Voices winner, and *Crying at the Movies* was a Minnesota Book Award finalist. In addition, she has received awards from the Bush Foundation, The Loft, and the National Endowment for the Arts. Her memoir *Great River Road: Memoir and Memory* is forthcoming from New Rivers Press. For more information see her website: www.madelonsprengnether.com.